THE BEES KNEES

— Stride —

THE BEES KNEES

compiled by

Gary Boswell

THE BEES KNEES

First edition 1990

ISBN 0 946699 87 9

Published by
STRIDE
37 Portland Street
Exeter
Devon
EX1 2EG
England

Printed in Great Britain by
Billing & Sons Ltd, Worcester

Foreword

What's so special about the bees knees
what's so special about them ?

I've got a spider with incredible ankles
and a budgie whose bellybutton's a genuine gem

Nobody raves about them

it's the same old over and again story
of the bee getting all the glory

*

One of the great things about STRIDE is that here, everybody is the bees knees. Everybody is special and everybody gets chance to share their work and their talents.
I am very proud to have been asked to compile this book and it is my greatest privilege to be able to introduce you to twelve poets whose poems you may not have had chance to read before.
Many of the poets I have met through the Poem-Swop Postal Writing Scheme — a great poet's playground that has writing pouring through your letterbox every day. You'll find details of how to join at the end of the book.
And if you do join, look out for my name on the Poem-Swop list and send me a Swop. I look forward to that.
For now, I present you with the first of many books that STRIDE are planning to do with poem-swoppers in the near future. I hope you enjoy it. Your poems may be in the next one, for here at STRIDE, you too are THE BEES KNEES!

Gary Boswell
September 1990

Contents

Lemn Sissay

LACK DOORS
THE MAN ON THE MOON
AIRMAIL TO A DICTIONARY
HOLMFIRTH IN THE MORNING
THE POWER OF PREJUDGEMENT
GOLD FROM THE STONE
AFRICAN CARNAGE

Sue Westcott

STAR
TIGER LILY
THE FIRST STEP
MRS FOX
SHANDY

Angela Topping

AND BOB'S YOUR UNCLE
WITCH IN THE SUPERMARKET
DID YOU WASH YOUR DIRTY NECK ?
THE FIRST FIVE METRES
PHOTOGRAPH DAY
THE FOREST OF MIRACLES

Gary Boswell

DADDY LONG LEGS MAN
A VOICE IN THE POCKET
our fish and chip shop's...
there was an old woman lived in a shoe...
R-R-R-R-R R R ROLLING IN THE AISLES
SUNDAY MORNING AT LAUGHARNE ESTUARY
one day soon...
A SHAME

Rita Ray

CAT'S EYES TIGER'S EYES
KITE FLYING DAY
ON THURSDAY MORNING
IT'S MY TURN FOR THE KOKORIKO
HOLIDAY WEATHER
DONKEY RIDE
A DICTIONARY OF SNOW
DEAR SANTA...

John Calvert

THE DAY THE SUPER-HEROES SOLD OUT
COUNTING SHEEP IN SUSSEX
THE ASCO SAINWAYS CHAIN STORE MASSACRE
...OR TAKE AWAY
THE PHANTOM LORRY OF THE A7
RAIN IN THE COUNTRY

Carole Pelling

NOT YET
AUNTIE WINNIE'S SUNDAY TEA
GOLDFISH BLUES
DARK IN THE PARK
THE INVISIBLE WOMAN
MY HERO
MISTER PHOTO-GRAPHER MAN

Phil Whitehead

SNOW
MINAMOTO – YORITOMO'S DREAM
in the Hankyu Department Store
THE CRACK OF THE SMACK AND THE PATIENT VOICE
SHARKS IN THE SWIMMING POOL

Rupert Loydell

MORNING POEM
PEBBLE
HOLIDAY SNAPS
DUSTBIN DAY
R.I.P.

DALEKS ON RAMSAY STREET

There's daleks down on Ramsay Street
They've vaporised little Jane,
AND Beverley, Jim and Helen.
You won't see them again.

Henry watches, devastated,
While Harold and Madge
Get EXTERMINATED

Bronwyn shouts,
"Sharon! Behind you mate.
There's a dalek coming!"
ZAZAZAZAZA – Too late.

The rest of the cast are running.
Just hear those aussie feet,
Racing for the safety
Of Coronation Street.

Now Ramsay Street is silent;
Not one character left alive.
What will they do
With the show half way through
And it's only five forty-five?

Not to worry.
Here's a brand new show.
'The Daleks of Ramsay Street',
Off we go.

(Now you and your friends can have lots of fun acting out your favourite scene from 'Neighbours', as if you were daleks)

John Coldwell

NeighBOOM
MONDAY
BBC1

SOCKS.

On Monday we wear quiet socks
Not flash, bang start a riot socks,
Not, Hey you come and try it socks.
On Monday we wear quiet socks.

On Tuesday we wear plain socks,
Not crazy and insane socks,
Not frazzle up your brain socks.
On Tuesday we wear plain socks.

On Wednesday we wear boring socks,
Not pass to me goal scoring socks,
Not Pollocks abstract drawing socks.
On Wednesday we wear boring socks.

On Thursday. Ordinary Socks,
Not horror, shock and scary socks,
Not beastly monsters hairy socks.
On Thursday. Ordinary socks.

On Friday, it's polite socks,
Not glowing in the night socks,
Not give your aunt a fright socks.
On Friday it's polite socks.

At weekends we wear loud socks,
That stand out in the crowd socks
And make our feet feel proud socks.
At weekends we wear loud socks.

John Coldwell

THE REPAIR MAN

He said that he had patched it
As best he could.
But, he warned,
Eventually the whole lot would have to come down.

He tucked his ladder under his arm
And pressed into my hand
A splintered shard of sky.

John Coldwell

POYTREE

Mr Graves told us in the morning
That we were going to have
POYTREE
in the afternoon,
with Mr. Adler.

So we lined up,
after break,
outside Mr Adler's classroom.
"What's POYTREE?" we asked each other.
Dopey Pete reckoned his Dad had got one
growing in his back garden.
Natalie thought that she had driven through it
on holiday in Cornwall.
I wished I could have been there too.
Know-All Jennifer,
said that it was a special
handicraft,
like basket weaving.
"Whatever it is," said Michael,
"It must be very important if you have to
go to Mr Adler for it."
POYTREE turned out to be Mr Adler
slapping our heads with a blue book,
instead of his usual red one.

Then Mr Adler read from the blue book.
His voice went sort of dreamy
and he had this funny smile on his face
like he knew something that you didn't.
I couldn't understand a word.
I looked at the others.
Michael's mouth hung open
So did Dopey Pete's
(but that's nothing to go by).
Even Jennifer was finding it hard to look clever.

Then I noticed Natalie.
She was smiling.
At me!
I smiled back.
We sat like that for all of POYTREE.

"There," said Mr. Adler like he hadn't breathed for ten minutes,
"That was POYTREE."

Then we put our chairs up and went home.

John Coldwell

MR JONES VERSUS ANGELA – BREAKTIME TUESDAY.

Bip Bip Bip

Mr. Jones: Into the playground everybody.
Angela: I need to read the noticeboard, sir.
Mr. Jones: Not Now. Out you go.
Angela: It's about a sports meeting, sir.
Mr. Jones: Lunchtime. Thursday. Now out you go.
Angela: And The stamp Club.
Mr. Jones: After school. Tuesday. Out you go.
Angela: I've left my apron in science.
Mr. Jones: It can stay there. Out you go.
Angela: I need to put my bag in maths.
Mr. Jones: Certainly not. Out you go.
Angela: Collect my art folder.
Mr. Jones: No. Out you go.
Angela: See the Head.
Mr. Jones: He's out. Out.
Angela: Miss Jones.
Mr. Jones: Out.
Angela: Mr Harvey.
Mr. Jones: Out.
Angela: The Caretaker.
Mr. Jones: Out.
Angela: I've got stomach ache.
Mr. Jones: Out.
Angela: But.
Mr. Jones: Out.
Angela: Sir.
Mr. Jones: Out.
Angela: Oh.
Mr. Jones: Out! Out! Out!

Bip. Bip. Bip.

Mr. Jones: Right everybody. In you come.

John Coldwell

A SURPRISE FOR GERALD THE SLOTH

It was in the bathroom
That Gerald the Sloth
Saw himself in the mirror
For the first time.
He was astounded.
The youthful glint in his eyes,
The glistening sheen of his fur,
The gentle curve of his powerful claws.

Gerald the Sloth was moved.
Moved to write poetry.
Poetry that would celebrate
His great beauty.

He wasted no time.
Out the bathroom,
Down the stairs,
Through the kitchen,
On his bike,
Down the road,
W.H. Smiths,
Stationery Department,
One pencil,
Note book,
Paid cash.
Then
On his bike,
Up the road,
Through the kitchen,
Up the stairs,
Into the bathroom.

Gerald the Sloth
Saw himself in the mirror
For the second time.
He was even more astounded.
Eyes; dull and blood-shot.
Fur; grey and thinning.
Claws; twisted and feeble.

Twenty five years is a long time.

John Coldwell

CARNIVAL FIASCO

I went to the carnival
My Mummy took me there
She made me wash behind my ears – even comb my hair
A massive bow in turquoise,
stuck upon my head
My dress with loads of sequins, polka dots in red.

I walked up to the mirror
to have a little look.
And oh! how I was shaken
I got a terrible shock.

I know my mum tries her utmost best
to have me look a treat.
But she doesn't have to face my friends who meet me
on the street.

I try my best to ruffle, my hair into a style
I stand there prim and proper forcing up a smile
My mother grins so proudly
She thinks I'm her delight
But she's not the one who has to look such an awful sight.

P Omoboye

INNOCENT UNTIL PROVEN GUILTY

Three Black youths, one the owner of a
car
followed by police, they won't get far
although quite innocent
and still not charged
the street is a courtroom
the Judge is the 'Sarge'

I was a witness
I naturally shook
my mind in turmoil, my body deep in
shock
I was a witness
I naturally shook
but all I could do was stand and look

Total provocation is what I saw
vicious manhandling and plenty more
shouting abuse — unnecessary force
police against black — naturally, of
course

Innocent bystanders shout in disgust
male onlookers join in the fuss
all quite reluctant, we view the situation
everybody anxious, we shake in
desperation

I was a witness
I tell no lies
seeing is believing
I heard the cries...

...I saw the young policeman, handcuffs
in hand
beating the head of an innocent man
I heard the yell, I could almost feel the
pain
as the weapon was lowered, again and
again

I was a witness, a witness I was
I saw the injustice take part in the 'Moss'
I saw the youths bundled in the van
dragged down the street like dogs — not
man
The sorrow I feel............
The hurt so real............

but only a witness what am I to do
but tell you the story so sad and true

P Omoboye

DAY CHAR VOUEZ ?

ITS SO STRANGE
I LOOK AT THE PICTURE
AND ALTHOUGH IT BARES NO RESEMBLANCE TO ME
THE CHILD IN THE MIDDLE
IS ME
I CAN SEE MYSELF   ALMOST FEEL MYSELF
ITS SO STRANGE
THOSE FRIENDS   ARE MY FRIENDS
THEIR SMILES   ARE MY SMILES
ITS ALMOST UNCANNY
BUT THE FEELINGS OF TOGETHERNESS
AND WHOLENESS ARE MINE

P Omoboye

(3x6)-(5x3

I KNOW THE ANSWER

Sir – Sir
I've got my hand up sir
I know the answer
But once again the teacher
ignores my urgent plea,
That the answer to that question
Has got to be – minus three

Sir I know the answer
His eyes glance above my head
Instead it's Tommy Tucker
who answers it, instead

'Who was the first man on the moon?'
ME Sir! me Sir! I Know! I Know!
SIT QUIET BOY!
Stop jumping about....
There is no need to shout
'The question Mark, is not referred to you....
Can you give me the answer Sue?
Clever girl – that is correct
NOW –
'Who knows where the highest mountain in the world is'?

Huh!
if he thinks I'm putting my hand up
He can get lost.
I won't give him the satisfaction
of telling me to sit down –
OK Mark – what's the answer?
Mark! – wake up Mark!
'In which country is the highest mountain?'
Me Sir? Do you mean me Sir?
eh! eh!
I don't know Sir.

P. Omoboye

MAKE YOUR MIND UP

When i talk
mum says i'm a chatterbox.
When i'm quiet
i'm in a mood.
When i nod
i'm being ignorant.
When i answer back i'm being rude.
When i sit still
i'm being boring.
When i run about
i'm a pain in the neck.
When i rush my dinner
i'm being greedy.
When i don't
my mother frets.

I very often wonder
if grown ups understand
if it's children that they really want
or robots to command.
Because everything i seem to do
i never get it right
the only option left to me
is to keep well out of sight.

I'm sure you've heard the phrase
"We should be seen and not be heard"
i think it would be worthy to add a teeny tiny word
"children should be children not be seen and not be heard".

P. Omoboye

A PRAISE POEM *(to be chanted out loud at the very tops of voices)*

Praise to fruit and veg, it keeps you healthy,
clean and fit.
Simon Pitt loves fruit and veg, and fruit and veg
loves Simon Pitt.

Praise to beans and cabbages and bucketfuls
of rice,
To carrots, spuds and scarlet runners, pepper,
salt and spice.
I love to sink my teeth into a giant juicy plum,
I like to eat fresh food because my best friend
is my tum.

Praise to fruit and veg, it keeps you healthy,
clean and fit.
Simon Pitt loves fruit and veg, and fruit and veg
loves Simon Pitt.

Onion, pumpkin, sweet potato, cauliflower and cole,
I'll eat them raw or fried or boiled or chopped
or sliced or whole,
Sprout and sauerkraut, leek and lettuce, parsnip
and parsley,
I'll buy them all in bulk; eat them for breakfast,
lunch and tea.

Peach and paw-paw, grape and grapefruit,
pear and mandarin,
Squidgy, squirty, succulent, the juice runs
down my chin,
Coconut and cantaloupe, current and cashew,
Fruit is fun, it's cheap and cheerful and
it's good for you...

Praise to fruit and veg, it keeps you healthy,
clean and fit.
Simon Pitt loves fruit and veg and fruit and veg
loves Simon Pitt.

Simon Pitt

MY TOUCAN THINKS HE'S INVISIBLE

My toucan thinks he's invisible. That bird is off his head,
It all began with a scientific journal that my toucan read.
He messed around with chemicals, he thought he'd break new gro
And now he thinks he's the only see-through bird for miles aroun

My toucan thinks he's invisible. He's got an evil mind,
He took a bus to Chester Zoo to see what he could find.
He sneaked into an aviary, crept up on a feeding dove,
They flung my toucan out on his ear, but the dove is now in love!

My toucan thinks he's invisible. He's such a stupid nerd,
There's far more sense in my little finger, than there is in
this feather-brained bird.
He took off all his feathers, and flew naked through the town,
A policeman called the army, and the army shot him down.

My toucan's flown to Heaven. My toucan's now a stiff.
That punky bird just dyed his feathers and greased them into a qu
He terrorises angels, hides their haloes, glues their wings.
But worst of all, my newly-departed toucan tries to sing;

"I used to be invisible. But now I'm only dead.
It's a pain in the neck, but I've got to get used to wearing shorts
in bed.
I'll go away now, and get some kip, 'cos tomorrow I've got to fly,
I've got a rendezvous with a pretty cockatoo at 'The Birdcage In
The Sky'!"

Simon Pitt

STAIN

Brushing won't do it
Scratching won't do it
Linseed oil won't do it
And neither will turps.

Soap won't do it
Water won't do it
A wet cloth won't do it
And neither will salt.

Vinegar won't do it
Lemon juice won't do it
Polish won't do it
And neither will spit.

You need a smile. Yes,
A smile will do the job
Just the thing
To remove that stain.

Simon Pitt

JANUARY

SUPERSNOUT !

My nose is gi-normous.

It's always the first bit of me to arrive.
People would cry, "Look, it's Jumbo!
He's looking this way – quick, duck!"
I hated my nose.
I spent a week with my nose immersed in the sink,
Hoping it would shrink.
I caught a gi-normous cold.

Then, one night, I dreamt I was asleep.
In my dream, I was woken up
By a strong smell of smoke.
I leapt out of bed, but there was no fire.

I followed the smell out of the house,
Down the street and across town.
With my giant nose twitching, I ran and ran,
Stopped to sniff, then ran some more.

At last, I halted outside the house
Of a very important person.
Smoke was seeping from under the door,
And dancing around the windows.

I telephoned the fire brigade,
They arrived just in time to save the very important person,
Who insisted on knighting my life-saving nose.
"Arise, Sir – er, Sniffer!"

Well, after that, I was hailed a hero,
A very important person.
The newspapers nicknamed me Supersnout.
Fans queued for miles to touch my nose.

I awoke from my dream
With a warm feeling inside.

Now, for the first time ever,
I want my nose to be seen.

You see,
There is nothing else quite like it,
or me,
in the entire universe.

So there!

Simon Pitt

WRAPPERS

The snow couldn't cover Dad's departing footsteps.
He left us:
Two confused children and a pale Mum.
I was offered the mantle of a man,
But swathed myself in silence.

On Christmas morning,
I tore away the wrappers from my pain,
And, unbowed, bawled down the wind,
I bawled down the wind, and everything.

Simon Pitt

HEY MISTER MISTER WHATCHA DOING TONIGHT?

I've been conned, I've been had,
They've found the poor sucker who would sell his own dad,
My pocket's been fleeced, I've been taken for a ride,
Taken to the cleaners, hung out and dried,
I put all my money on a one-legged horse,
There I was-watching it, hopping up the course,
Then came the knock on opportunity's door
I flung it wide open and this bloke who knew the score cried,

"Hey mister mister whatcha doing tonight?
We need a volunteer to referee the rhino fight!
We're looking for a chump to sell glasses to the blind
A certain simple someone with a peanut for a mind."
So I said "Yes, yes!" 'cos I like a quiet life,
I knew that I'd been conned 'cos my back was full of knife,
Some of us are born stupid, we simply have no choice,
But to reach for our wallets when we hear that sneaky voice;

"Pst! Hey, mister mister whatcha doing tonight?
We need a volunteer to find out if piranha really bite
There's money to be made from gluing leaves back on the trees,
You could wind up rich by selling honey to the bees."
I was the one who tried to teach a frog to croak,
The one who bought shares in the business that went broke,
The one who bought a cockerel, expecting it to lay,
The one who sang carols in the middle of May,
Then again came the thump on opportunity's door,
I flung it wide open, then just as before he said,

"Hey mister mister whatcha doing tonight?
We need a volunteer to paintspray all the pillar boxes white,
We want a likely sort of lad to make the Mona Lisa frown,
Someone to stop the traffic in the middle of town,
A three-legged man to run the two-legged race,
An ambitious type to put Mike Tyson in his place"
I said "Please go away – why can't you let me be?
There are millions of other suckers, why choose me?"
He brought his face close up to mine and fixed me with a stare
and said: "True but the SUPER SUCKER's very, very rare!"

Simon Pitt and Gary Boswell

BAG LADY

she looks like a pile of
discarded rugs

like a jumble sale
when the dealers have gone

she sits in a huddle
beside the town hall

always alone

sits on the pavement with
her back against the wall

the bag lady, the bag lady
misfit in our city

the bag lady, the bag lady
got no place in society

in the town centre she
sits solid as a queen

wonder where she came from
wonder what she's seen

was she born a bag baby
what has she been

this bag lady
bag lady
                    bag lady.

Joan Poulson

WITH MY WHACKER-PLATE

all day long I walk
with my whacker-plate
around and about the
busy streets of town

all day me and my jazz-
jumpy whacker-plate
crush and crunch the stones
in the pavements down

all day I stomp with my
biff-bumpy whacker-plate
flattening and smoothing
the lumps from the ground

but at night I wander
to the surfy moonlit
strand, cliff-clumpy with
my whacker-plate

jigger-jagger whacker-
plate. and together
we pound pebbles
into fine, moon-silver sand.

Joan Poulson

COPING

how would *you* like it –
if you had five brothers
if you were left-handed
if your mother's ambition
was to be a clown
if your hair slithered down
in greasy strands
sandy-red
if everything you said
came out in a lisp
because you had to
wear a brace
if you were the only one in
your year to live
miles out of town
if you had a face that was a
smear of orange freckles

how do I cope, I ask myself!
I suppose it's because I am amazing –
simply amazing.

Joan Poulson

INSIDE-OUT

I stride down the street
and

kick a can

swing across the road
beyond the
lollipop man

ignore all the kids
from the other
side of town

keep my eyes ahead

wear a slight frown

keep my eyes ahead
repeating
repeating
repeating in my head
'stay cool! stay cool!
they can all drop dead!'

with my streetwise swagger
I pass them every day
don't let anything
give me away

not a suspicion
never let them see
the differences
the differences
the differences
between

the inside
the outside
inside-out
of me.

Joan Poulson

GRANDAD'S DINNERS

grandad says he likes
a big dinner

grandma says he's
getting fat

she tells him he
should try to be thinner

grandad says
"Tell that to the cat!"

Joan Poulson

GIRLS ARE LIKE DIAMONDS

(for Sarah)

Girls are understanding
and if you've got a problem
will soon find a way to sort
things out, show you that life's
okay, make you laugh, take
another look at your day.

Girls don't waste time
complaining, are efficient
at getting things done. And
afterwards, know how to
relax, enjoy life, have fun.

Girls smell nice, not
sweatiness masked with Old
Spice. They are capable, make
looking great with no money
a breeze, turn jumble sale
stuff into pleasing and
trendiest clothes.

Girls are like diamonds,
shining in so many ways, in
science, in commerce, with
people or food. They are
sensitive, tune in to others
as if on a radio wave, which
saves *them* from sinking when
life seems unfair for there's
always another girl ready to
share, who knows what you feel,
helps you back on your feet,
ready, if trembling, to re-face
the world. And I'm glad –
HOW I'M GLAD I'M A GIRL.

Joan Poulson

"YOU'RE RIGHT," SAID GRANDAD.

I went round to help him
the day he moved
it was an upstairs flat
this old one he had
he'd lived there
with Gran
for twenty-nine years
they told him
it was time
he had a move

we laughed, me and Grandad
at the dark front room
"Like an old fox's den,"
I said. "Just wait until
you're sitting in that bright
light room – with all
that glass. You'll be able to
sit and watch
everybody pass."
"You're right, I will,"
said Grandad.

we laughed, me and Grandad
at the garden round the back.
"Like a jungle, at its best,"
I said. "Just wait until
you're resting in your
new place. No more
hacking-out
a deckchair space.
No weeds annoying you.
There'll be plenty
company for you, too.
They'll sit outside
the people from
the other bungalows.
sit on the benches
chat with you."
"You're right, they will,"
said Grandad.

We laughed, me and Grandad
at his rickety old shed.
"Like something from
a horror film!" I said.
"You'll be much better off
without it. And didn't
the doctor tell you
all that sawdust
wasn't good, got on your chest?
And we've all got wooden stools
and things, enough to last
a lifetime, anyway.
Our Sheryll really loved
that box you made her.
All those different
colours, different woods.
Dad says you've been a
first-rate craftsman
in your time."
"He's right, I have,"
said Grandad.
"Yes, I have."

Joan Poulson

SNAKE

she lies still
seemingly serene
her body firm
surprising
dryly draped
around my arm

muscle-machine

unblinkingly
she suffers
my exploring touch
finger-tips
that hesitantly
trace the polished
pattern
of her scales

tessellation

caress
her pale
cool skin
smooth
as fresh-planed
sycamore

press gently
on her marbled side
then press again
amazed
by her solidity
and she slides
glides
sleekly to my shoulder

glossed fluidity

sensational.

Joan Poulson

LACK DOORS

A perplex palace
Doctor Who has gone
I unveil the new tardis
By British Telecom

Replied a Timelord
I travel no more
It is untoward
The lack of a door.

Lemn Sissay

IT'S FOR YOU

THE MAN ON THE MOON

He collects the daylight
Shuffles it into his pockets
And wellington boots
Down his pants and
In the lining of his suit

He scrapes it from leaves
wet from the rain
Licks it off windows
And with a small spoon he scoops it
From the edge of the shadows

He puts three mirrors
At the foot of his house
And every single morning
He would strip the sunrise from the mirrors
And catch some more by yawning

Then he'd race to each doorstep
And take the bottle tops
Tiptoe through the gate
Run into the valley
And skim the sun from the lake

But, his real work begins
In the darkest night
This is when he flies
To a white shaped rock
In the centre of the sky

He takes the sun from out of his pockets
In bottle tops and silver lockets
Pulls his arm right back
and throws it into the black
Like fireworks it sprays the midnight gloom
The light at night is from the man on the moon.

Lemn Sissay

AIRMAIL TO A DICTIONARY

Black is...the shawl of the night
Secure from sharp paranoic light

Black is...the pupil of the eye
Putting colour in the sea's skin and earthen sky

Black is...the oil of the engine
On which this whole world is depending

Black is...light years of space
Holding on its little finger this human race

Black is...the colour of ink
That makes the history books we print

Black is...the colour of coal
Giving work to the miners, warmth to the old

Black is...the army. Wars in the night
Putting on the Black to hide the white

Black is...the strip on my cardcash
That lets me get money from the Halifax

Black is...the eclipse of the sun
displaying its power to every one

Black on Black is Black is Black
Strong as asphalt and tarmac

Black is...a word that I love to see.
Black is that, yeah, Black is me.

Lemn Sissay

HOLMFIRTH IN THE MORNING

The sky creeps up the hillside
And tickles from the edge
The Black crow hitches a free ride
From a tree swallowing ledge

No green is the same green
Nor no knife blade of grass
The diamond dew it seems
That hangs like cut crystal glass

Rich as a soldier in myth
And all tales carry weight
Each hillside a precious gift
Holmfirth at eight.

Lemn Sissay

THE POWER OF PREJUDGEMENT

You say I am a lying child
I say I'm not
You say there you go again

You say I am a rebellious child
I say no I'm not
You say there you go again

Quite frankly mum
I've never seen a rebellious child before
And when my mates said
Jump in that puddle and race you through the park
(y'know the muddy one)
I didn't think about the mud

When you said 'why are you dirty!'
I could feel the anger in your voice
I still don't know why

I said 'I raced my mates through the park'
You said it was deliberate
I said I didn't, I mean I did, but it wasn't
You said I was lying
I said no I am not
You said there you go again

Later in the dawn of adolescence
It was time for my leave
I with my suitcase social worker
You with your husband,
walked our sliced ways

Sometimes I would run back to you
Like a child through a muddy park
With adult achievements tucked under my arm
Then I'd explain them with a child like twinkle in my eye
Thinking any mother would be proud...

Your eyes, desperately trying to be wise and unrevealing
revealed all
Still you fell back into the heart of the same rocking chair

Saying There you go again

And I did

And I have

Lemn Sissay

GOLD FROM THE STONE
(dedicated to Valerie Bloom)

Water cupped in hands
Taken from the stream
Brought upon a laughing land
Through the mouth of a scream

Gold from the stone
Oil from the earth
I yearned for my home
From the time of my birth

Strength of a mother's whisper
Shall carry me until
The hand of my lost sister
Joins onto my will

Root to the earth
Blood from the heart
Could never from birth
Be broken apart

Food from the platter
Water from the rain
The subject and the matter
I'm going home again

Can't sell a leaf to a tree
Nor the wind to the atmosphere
I know where I'm meant to be
And I can't be satisfied here

Can't give light to the moon
Nor mist to the drifting cloud
I shall be leaving here soon
Costumed cultured and crowned

Can't give light to the sun
Nor a drink to the sea
The earth I must stand upon
I shall kiss with my history

Sugar from the cane
Coal from the wood
Water from the rain
Life from the blood

Gold from the stone
Oil from the earth
I yearned for my home
Ever since my birth

Food from the platter
Water from the rain
The subject and the matter
I'm going home again

Lemn Sissay

AFRICAN CARNAGE

And did the children
Throwing sticks and stones
And walk did the children
Skin and bones
And walk did the children
Chanting verse
And walk did the children
As if they were cursed
And walk did the children
Cut and Bruised
And walk did the children
Frustrated, confused
And walk did the children
Sister and Brother
And walk did the children
And ran did the children
Stopped playing in sand
And ran did the children
Hand in Hand
And ran did the children
To the top of the hill
And shout did the children
''We have a will, we have a will''
And killed were the children.

Lemn Sissay

STAR.

In a sky so black
it's blue,
a white star dot
shines.
Pin-pointed brilliance.
A silent,
solitaire,
of light.

Sue Westcott

TIGER LILY

Its vivid brightness stuns.
Revealing
a spattering of ink dots.
Arched, curling petals
stretch and bend.
Opening wide,
the delicate, orange
softness,
explodes in my eyes.

Sue Westcott

THE FIRST STEP

The new boy walks into the room.
Suddenly, from noisy chaos
there is silence
as staring pairs of eyes
focus on him.
He hesitates and wonders,
'Why do they look at me
as if I am an alien?
Have I got two heads, six legs
or is my hair blue?'
The new boy inhales deeply
gathering up his courage
and steps into their domain,
He remembers his mum's words,
"Be friendly,"
So he attempts a smile.
Shy and thin it slides across
his paper white face.
"Hi," he softly speaks a whisper.
"My name is Brian."
And a flashing flood of
dazzling white greets him!

Sue Westcott

MRS FOX.

John's Mum, Mrs. Fox,
You know,
comes into school
to teach us to sew.
And she hears readers,
things like that.
Though yesterday
she ended up flat
on her back.
Down, down she went
all limp on the floor.
Our teacher had never seen
anything like it before.
All because of Linda
who had been using a knife
on her right thumb,
she'd cut quite a slice.
A pin prick of blood
was all to be seen
yet poor Mrs. Fox
turned instantly green.
She moaned and she groaned
way down on the floor.
All Linda could say
was, "My finger is sore."
Frightened Fredrica had shouted
"She's dead!"
So Tell Tale Georgina
rushed off for the head,
who came with a run
Panting, way out of breath
expecting to see a tragic death.
Yet there was Mrs Fox
all pale and white
with large round eyes
still filled with fright.

Our teacher did help her
up on her feet
and kindly suggested
she missed it next week.
So poor Mrs Fox
just nodded her head
and rushed off home
and straight into bed!

Sue Westcott

SHANDY

I wasn't there when my dog died.
I was away on holiday
enjoying myself.
I didn't know
my dog lay in pain
whilst I was having fun.
I came home full to the brim
with seaside tales.
Yet I didn't know she'd
been taken to the vets.
All I knew she wasn't there to greet me.
No soft, paw prints on the floor.
No warm, wet, shuffling nose.
I wasn't there when my dog died.
I feel full of guilt deep inside
because I didn't have time to say goodbye.

Sue Westcott

AND BOB'S YOUR UNCLE

I

No he's not! Not quick either.
Like Jesus, comes at Christmas.
Not a knee to climb on,
Nor cheek to kiss: He's Mr Alty,
Someone to thank for the hard
Jigsaw or glossy book
With pages stiff enough
To cut a thumb. Above my head
A table set with turkey salad,
Mince pies, piled and sugar-dusted,
And, iced in secret, gaudy cake.

II

Remember mother dotting with cherries,
Sprinkling hundreds and thousands,
Beckoning to whisper 'Go
And talk to Bob.'? Not Mr Alty anymore
Though he's the same bewildered man,
Who had been altered, dazed for life:
A hand grenade blew up in his face,
Obliterating all his dreams; his fiancee
Married someone else. It was easier
To talk to him before I knew. His eyes
Struggle behind spectacles that never
Bring a sharpening. I search for words
To show I'm here
                    but can't begin.

III

Last night we drove through the darkening streets
Of a home town left behind ten years ago.
I saw his uncertain figure listening for
A gap in traffic, turning this way and that.

But it's too late now... those Christmas teas
When he'd bring round his home-made wine
Have yielded to bleaker rituals.
Chastened by losses of my own, I know
No words of mine could waken more
Than his tongue-tying 'yes, mmm.'

Angela Topping

INSTANT
BAT

WITCH IN THE SUPERMARKET

There's a witch in the supermarket over there
After Fowler's treacle for her flyaway hair,
Buying up nail-varnish — black or green?
Rooting in the freezer for toad ice-cream!

There's a witch in the supermarket next row on
Asking where the Tinned Bats' Ears have gone,
Mutters 'Why do they always change things round?
Mouse Tails and Rat's Tongues can't be found!'

There's a witch in the supermarket down that aisle
Searching for something to blacken her smile,
She's a trolley full of tins for her witch's cat
Who simply swears by Bit-o-Bat.

Times are difficult and Bovril has to do
Instead of newt's blood for a tasty stew;
Sun-dried blue-bottles crunchy and sweet
Desiccated spiders for a Hallowe'en treat.

There's a witch in the supermarket at the till
Scribbling her cheque with a grey goose quill!
There's a witch at the check-out, look, mum, quick!
Piling up her shopping on a big broomstick!

Angela Topping

DID YOU WASH YOUR DIRTY NECK?

Did you wash your dirty neck?
Did you heck!

Did you wash your dirty cheeks?
Not for weeks!

Did you wash your dirty nose?
I suppose!

Did you wash your dirty hair?
That I can't bear!

Did you wash your dirty brow?
Show me how!

Did you wash your dirty head?
Stayed in bed!

Did you wash your dirty legs?
In scrambled eggs!

Did you wash your dirty thigh?
With a sigh!

Did you wash your dirty ears?
Not for years!

Angela Topping

THE FIRST FIVE METRES

Wanting too much, I feared
The spat of blood, counted
Weeks to twenty-eight.

A long journey, and now,
She's washed up in my arms,
Small survivor, snuggled in wool.

Her eyes question everything:
The ticking nurses,
New father's beard.

She tongues the nipple,
Half-interested, while her eyes
Study the window's blank rectangle.

Unclasped from babyhood,
Seven years of questions
Fizz her eyes today,

Launching herself into water
Without armbands for the first time,
Swimming, swimming away.

Angela Topping

PHOTOGRAPH DAY

A knot of mothers is drawn tight.
Their children fray their nerves, unravel them.
They wait for the canvas pavilion,
A camera on its tripod and a giddy photographer.

Captured on film is a moment
Where no party is progressing
And the pintucked child is smiling
From no particular happiness
And at no one but the photographer.

Angela Topping

THE FOREST OF MIRACLES

For David

There is a forest deep in Russia:
The Forest of Miracles.
Tall pines stretch limbs
Oaks straddle leaf-mould.

The forest is Forbidden,
And men may forage only briefly there,
Muffled in masks, their geiger counters bleeping
Signalling to each other through antique silence.

Now strange shapes sprout;
The wrong leaves and convoluted growths
Whisper shady secrets.
The crunch of pine-needles
Is deadly – and the toadstools.

Angela Topping

You've bowed to Batman
You've gawped at Elephant man
You've shrieked at Spiderman
now, be totally bemused by
DADDY LONG LEGS MAN !!!!!!!

(cue intro music over which is sung;

"He's got ninety degree knees.
elongated elbows. Like a hooligan's
helicopter flying upside down.

DADDY LONG LEGS MAN – fearlessly waltzing
straight into windows
DADDY LONG LEGS MAN – scrawny superhero who
is constantly concussed
DADDY LONG LEGS MAN – hiccup hopping through
the dangers of the night
Whenever you're in trouble just switch on the
light,
he'll come a dangling.")

This week's story line;

There was trouble off the Irish coast. A trawler trappe on raging rocks. The sea snarling like a trussed up tiger. Lifeboats already los Underwriters counting costs. A story specially staged for the front page of th Sun (a not very bright newspaper).

Without warning. Terrorist intervention. Million megaton bomb. God (newly elected president) put his foot down. Hurled in Hurricane. Tossed in a tornado. Engineered an earthquake all down the Melling Road.

Things were getting out of hand.
Only one option open.
Send for
DADDY LONG LEGS MAN!!!!!!

He ambled in on the Western wind (saving strain on his wafery wings) – bumped into the beacon that was by now burnt to a cinder and dangled somewhat dizzily above the holocaust happening below.

HELLO MUM
90°
HOOL

"Blimey" he said after an astute assessment of the situation, "This calls for the big slipper".

Not moving as quickly as one would have hoped in suc a crisis, Daddy Long Legs man went off to the planet Cocoonius to fetch the big slipper. On the way, he bumped into the Sun (a very bright planet) and was delayed for several hours whilst he rematerialised himself. That done, he hauled the big slipper onto his fragile back and carried it all the way to earth (thus earning hero status again).

As he entered earth's atmosphere, he swung back the slipper and swatted sensationally, managing to squash the entire planet flat against the universe floor. And so the earth became two dimensional at last (admittedly with little spindly bits sticking out all over. These became know as the Planks, and in the new order, criminals were asked to walk along them If they fell off the end, they were witches.)

Daddy Long Legs man was hailed as a not quite so clumsy superhero as had at first been thought and lived simply and contentedly thereafter, the happy ending spoiled only by the news that Richard Attenborough forgot to load the film into his camera.

Re cue intro music and re sing intro song
finishing with a subtle fade out.

Gary Boswell

A VOICE IN THE POCKET

A friend of mine lost his voice.

"Will you help me look for it?" he said.

"Pardon." we replied.

He told us again using his hands.
We understood and started to help
looking for it.

We looked everywhere.
That is, we looked nowhere.
Where do you start looking for a voice?

"Better off listening for it."

It was my brother who came up with
that clever conclusion.

So we all closed our eyes
and started the search.

We listened everywhere.
Up the chimney (I got soot in my ear)
In the Wastepaper bin (my brother got sellotape stuck to his nose)
Under the carpets
inside the cushions
on top of the wardrobe
and over the hills.

The lost voice was nowhere to be heard.

My friend sat down with a face about
to crumple into cry when instead it lurched
sideways into foolish grin.

"Guess what," he said "I've found it. It was in
my pocket all the time."

Gary Boswell

Our fish and chip shop's
got an aquarium fitted in the corner
filled with a whole load of multi-coloured Flashing Fish.

It's called the underwater disco
by a few of the locals who've noticed
that it looks like an underwater disco.
It does.

And there's a story round our way
told by a fella who says that one night,
when he was in,
he saw a chip swimming round
in the underwater disco.

We asked him what colour the chip was
and he said he didn't know.

Which is why we think it's not true.

Gary Boswell

There was an old woman lived in a shoe
spent her entire life
going round
saying

"Poooooh!"

Gary Boswell

R-R-R-R-R-R-R-ROLLING IN THE AISLES

Between the beans and the jeans
it hits you
Beneath the bleach that's out of reach
you'll feel it booming from above
When you're stood staring at tomatoes
wondering if they'll blend with boiled banana
While baby's breaking biscuits in his basket just for fun

That's when it happens.
That's when the microphonic witch
in the Watch tower switches on.
The British Shopping Public dive for shelter under shelves:

"Ming.Mong. Would Mister R-R-R-R-R-R-Roosburger R-R-R-R-Roll
along to R-R-R-R-R-Reception R-R-R-R-R-R-Right away."

It's weird to feel like you've been shot
by what someone had to say.

Clutching your left pocket,
the one that holds your wallet,
you stagger to the supervisor
to see if she can stop the bleeding:

she's just about to tell you
there's nothing wrong except baby (he needs feeding)
when the second wave advances:

"Would Miss R-R-R-R-R-R-Roofr-r-r-r-Raiser R-R-R-R-R-Run
along R-R-R-R-R-R-Rapidly to R-R-R-R-R-Returned Goods to
R-R-R-R-R-Rectify a Wr-R-R-R-R-Rongdoing!"

*

When we realise it's not the Mafia
mowing down the masses
but some dentist's dummy
with her machined gums
and teeth that keep
getting stuck in traffic,
we feel relieved

d a little cheated

d go back uncertainly to grumbling
out the rising price
short grain rice
d a society
it's crumbling
the second.

's not safe to walk the streets. Be the last straw if it
sn't safe to do the shopping."

*

nce went for a job in
s super shop:

t-time
rieving trolleys
m ponds
t off the ring road.

ere was me and this other fella being interviewed:

"Names ? "

id: "Gary Boswell."
e other
la said: "Rudolf Raspberry-Ripple."

e interviewer looked up with one o' them looks.
new I might as well have gone home there and then
t I stayed for the experience of interview technique
d the off-chance that maybe Rudolf Raspberry-Ripple
uld drop dead.

t he didn't.
d when we were introduced to the rest of the staff:

his is Mister R-R-R-R-R-Richards from R-R-R-R-R-Retail,
R-R-R-R-R-Ron R-R-R-R-R-R-Rockafella from R-R-R-R-Rudimentary
ance, Mister and Missus R-R-R-R-R-R-Rhubarb (registry wedded),

R-R-R-R-R-R-Robert R-R-R-R-R-Rooftiler in charge of cross-
R-R-R-R-R-R-Referencing, R-R-R-R-R-Ruby R-R-R-R-R-Ratatouille,
R-R-R-R-R-R-R-Reginald R-R-R-R-R-Rottweiler and Mister
R-R-R-R-R-R-R-R-Ranjit R-R-R-R-R-R-Ribena-addict from
R-R-R-R-R-R-R-Records."

that's when the final resignation sank in.

I turned to Rudolf and wished him all the luck
in the R-R-R-R-R-Refridgerator
and left
to pursue
a
career
in
WRiting —

a word which as you can see has had a safety W put on its front to stop
it from R-R-R-R-R-R-Rolling in the aisles!!!

Gary Boswell

SUNDAY MORNING AT LAUGHARNE ESTUARY

a broccoli barrow
a spithead of sprouts
a brown sea of gravy
swirling in over yorkshire
pudding sand.
The meat is missing.

I tell a lie.

There in the thick white line
of horseradish detergent that
comes in each night on the gravy tide
rolls the pale white head of the company director
who's fallen off his water skis and is taking
the opportunity for a first hand look at the
levels of pollution (he's up to his neck in it)

before lunch.

Gary Boswell

One day soon, a fella came along with his loud-hailer and announced:

"That's it. That's all there is."

We didn't take much notice. Even though he'd had a loud-hailer, he hadn't said it very loud.

We saw him again on the television news. On his own. Just him. And all he had to say was:

"That's it. That's all there is."

Only this time he added a bit more.

"There's no more. You'll have to do without."

We looked around for Nicholas Wychell. He wasn't around. When our fella disappeared off the screen, nothing else ever came on to it ever again.

There was a picture of our fella on the front page of the last ever newspaper. And a headline in speech marks that said the same as he'd said on last night's T.V. News.

"THAT'S IT. THAT'S ALL THERE IS. THERE'S NO MORE. YOU'LL HAVE TO DO WITHOUT."

There didn't seem much point switching on the telly to watch nothing so instead, we plugged in an oak tree and for forty years, the three of us sat and watched it grow.

Gary Boswell

A SHAME—

I wrote a poem

about the wind.
I can't show it you though

It blew away.

Gary Boswell

CAT'S-EYES TIGER'S-EYES

I came to this school yesterday
I brought my bag of marbles
Cat's-eyes, tiger's-eyes, big silver alleys

No-one talked to me at first
just looked me up and down
Cat's-eyes, tiger's-eyes, big silver alleys

Then Wayne with spiky hair said
"Play you for keeps?"
Cat's-eyes, tiger's-eyes, big silver alleys

Play me for keeps
with my own bag of marbles?
Cat's-eyes, Tiger's-eyes, big silver alleys

There's something wrong here
I can't fall for that
Cat's-eyes, tiger's-eyes, big silver alleys

A girl came along
offered me a cheesy crisp
Cat's-eyes, tiger's-eyes, big silver alleys

"Go away," she said to Wayne
"Go and cheat the big boys"
Cat's-eyes, tiger's-eyes, big silver alleys

She played with me all playtime
and very soon I lost all my
Cat's-eyes, tiger's-eyes, big silver alleys

Rita Ray

KITE FLYING DAY

They are all up now
kestrels, eagles, insects
with compound eyes
flapping fringed butterflies
mathematical miracles
multifaceted
inflatable rockets
trailing plastic flames
psychedelic pink and green
punky stunters
each tugging at a piece of sky

A deep cobalt fish
waving red paper fins
swims snakily by
through the blue air
crosses lines brings them down
one by one
wheels and spins as he gains
the sky space for himself

Tracing back the line
we find no one
at the end of his string

Rita Ray

ON THURSDAY MORNING

A
skein of
wild geese
strayed low
over Little
Hulton We
gazed up
amazed at
their grey
flap flapping
next year
at the
same time
I'll stand
here hoping

Rita R

IT'S MY TURN FOR THE KOKORIKO

David bangs a bongo
Rachel scrapes the guiro
Sammy rattles jingle sticks
and Sophie taps a tom tom

It's my turn for the kokoriko

Paul clashes cymbals
Sarah shakes the tubo
Carla clacks a chocolo
and Tammy twists the cabasa

It's my turn for the kokoriko

'You're not in time' says David
banging Rachel with the bongo
'Oh yes she is' cries Sophie
and taps him with her tom tom
Tammy twists Carla who clacks
Sammy with the chocolo
Paul clashes Sarah
Sarah shakes Rachel but..

It's my turn for the kokoriko

Rita Ray

HOLIDAY WEATHER

On an island of beach
donkeys shiver
gulls are blown sideways
slapping and flapping
children wearing macs
over psychedelic tee shirts
dig in the wet sand

Their blue-cheeked mothers
sit on towels on the steps
A dog's pawprint in the hard sand
fills with rain water
But look, it's brightening –
just a little

Rita Ray

DONKEY RIDE

My legs stretch wide
across the donkey's back
We go jangling and jogging
round the circle of sand
I love to touch his neck
he smells of old rugs and warm bread

Rita Ray

A DICTIONARY OF SNOW

The Eskimos
have lots of words
for snow

There's fine snow
thick snow
blizzard snow
snow for building igloos....

Here's my list of words
for snow
splatty is for making snowballs
swoooosh is for sledging through
skolOSH is for kicking with your wellies
smooolly lies on the pavement
                waiting for footprints
shlumpish goes up and down over grassy fields
                until birds make patterns in it
squalOOM is to skid along in the playground
                before the caretaker throws sand on it
skulptush packs together squeaking in your hands
                as you build a snowman

I still need words for the snow you wipe
off the tops of walls
as you run along the street
and for the sort that cakes
and melts on mittens
after a whole playtime

Rita Ray

TO
GRAN
XXX

DEAR SANTA...

We're having our chimney extended
It's going to be very wide
You see, Jim wants a rhino for Christmas
And we'll never get it inside

We must make the fireplace bigger
Or Santa will really be sorry
For dad wants a brand new back garden
While grandma has asked for a lorry

A million year old hairy mammoth
Is what our young Hilda would like
Cousin Randolph has always been boring
He only wants a new bike

Mum's set her heart on a castle
With gas central heating all through
Aunty Madge prefers Buckingham Palace
Complete with a gold plated loo

We've written our letters to Santa
And this morning he gave us a ring
Says he'll post all our presents next Wednesday
Then he's off to Marjorca till Spring.

Rita Ray

THE DAY THE SUPER-HEROES SOLD OUT

Reading through the Daily Planet one glorious morning
when – WHAM!
The headlines hit me like a
plateful of cold school semolina
SPLAT!
CAN THIS BE TRUE?
The Superheroes losing their identities
To take up day jobs – HOLY KRYPTONITE!
Quickly I read the rest of the article – using my X-Ray vision.
In disbelief I read...
SO FAR WE HAVE SEEN.

Iceman selling fridge-freezers in the electric showrooms
Spiderman spinning plastic mesh for fences
The Human Torch flogging fire extinguishers.

GOSH!
And all over Metropolis
Even to the outskirts of Gotham City
Superman showing how a man can fly
Batman and Robin demonstrating abseiling.
The Incredible Hulk showing off tear-resistant shirts.
WHATEVER NEXT?
ONE THING IS CLEAR
If the Superheroes cannot fight for justice
Then – ZAP!
I shall have to do it myself
Hiding my secret identity in a Debenham's carrier bag
I set off down the High Street, looking mean
In search of the nearest telephone box

John Calvert

NO SALES -MEN
H·TORCH
FIRE
SHERS

COUNTING SHEEP IN SUSSEX

(lullaby)

When it's bedtime out in Sussex
And the sun sets on the downs
When the South-East stars are shining
Over obscure little towns
All the farmers have it knitted
When they can't get to sleep
They just bide their time
With a little rhyme
Which they use to count their sheep:

one-erum, two-erum, cock-erum, shoe-erum, seth-erum, shath-erum,
whinberry, wagtail, tarry diddle, don.

Every ewe and ram they tot up
From Linch Down to Kithurst Hill
Cheaper than a mug of Horlicks
Better for you than a pill
If you're wide-eyed, if you're restless
No good staring at the clock
Make your thoughts a pen
Count Them up again
Your imaginary flock.

CHORUS

Let the hills become the pillows
In the landscape of your bed
When the sheepdog rounds the last strays
From the ceiling overhead
And the tinkly neck-bells call 'home'
As the night grows still and deep
Bringing peace of mind
Wagging tails behind
Out in Sussex, counting sheep.

CHORUS

John Calvert

THE ASCO SAINWAYS CHAIN STORE MASSACRE

First voice: PLEASE TAKE A BASKET
PLEASE TAKE A BASKET
OR USE A TROLLEY
OR USE A TROLLEY

Sugar, sardines, sausages, strawberries in syrup, salmon paste, shaving cream...

First voice: THIS WEEK'S SPECIAL OFFER
THIS WEEK'S SPECIAL OFFER

'''marmite, muesli, macaroni, margarine, milk...

A NEW LINE
A NEW LINE

...Bread, biscuits, beefstock cubes, butterscotch, bubble bath...

...'DIANA SMITH TO THE CHECKOUT, PLEASE'...

PACK OF FOUR
PACK OF TWO
GET ONE FREE

...cornflakes, crisps, cling-film, canned carrots, cocktail sticks...

Low Calorie
Low Fat

'STAFF ANNOUNCEMENT'... END OF FIRST LUNCH'

Win a holiday!
Win a Ford Fiesta!

'Scuse me, want to try a sample? It's cheese week'

'CATHY POLLARD TO THE CHECKOUT, PLEASE'.

Dog food, disposable nappies, dried fruit, disinfectant, double cream...

PLEASE RETURN YOUR TROLLEY
PLEASE RETURN YOUR TROLLEY

And

Help
Us
Keep
Prices
Down

John Calvert

...OR TAKE AWAY

When I walk into a chip shop
For a paper of chips and cod
There's always something struck me there
As being rather odd.

One thing I just can't understand
I don't know why or how
But the girl behind the counter
Always asks me, 'TO EAT NOW?'

Why does she always ask me THAT?
Perhaps it's not her fault
If she sprinkles on a question
With her vinegar and salt

Of course I want to eat them NOW
Tomorrow they'll be cold
But does it matter, either way
As long as they've been sold?

Course, if I waited 'til next week
I don't think I'd be able
To face their deep-fried greasiness
Across our breakfast table.

I think all chip shops in the land
From Inverness to Slough
Should tell their ladies, not to stand
And ask me, 'To eat now?'

John Calvert

THE PHANTOM LORRY OF THE A7

On an evening, when the sounds of day
Are dying — all is still
Behind the moon, the lorry
Comes over Watherston Hill

And as the darkness steals up
Over fountainhall and Stow
Along the old A7
By the water's tumbling flow

Now moving under quiet stars
Winding by the farms and fields
Heading North to Edinburgh
Heading South to Galasheils

Running silent, with no engine
Ghostly headlights probe the dark
Drifting down the empty hours
Phantom tyres leave no mark.

And yet old May said she'd seen it
Bowl along a grassy track
When the summer heat-haze hovered
Long before the nights turned black

Who could be the vehicle's driver?
Who could be the driver's mate?
Did they meet with dire disaster
On some far-forgotten date?

Do they ferry some strange cargo
To some place just known to them
Were they on a secret mission
Hidden from the eyes of men?

Now the spectral wheels are gliding
Through the hills, below the trees
By the slumbering Border villages
Where the closed eye never sees.

Travelling the dead-time highway
Driving moonlight miles of white
On to Heriot and fala
Goes the lorry through the night.

John Calvert

RAIN IN THE COUNTRY

One day of solid rain can drown the land
And make the snaking river break its chain
Can ruin new-stacked hay, turn field to swamp
Above the water, hedge and fence remain.

For hours now, in stair-rods from pencilled skies
The darkening hills are distanced and then lost
Those crowded cows are used to it by now
They stare it out – their hooves in churning clay.

John Calvert

NOT YET

Have you got any presents, yet?
Said the kitchen door
To the Birthday Boy
Who was nearly ten.

Just a joke book
From my Auntie Pat,
But I'm not ten yet
Not until Sunday afternoon.

The kitchen door yawned
And banged shut.

Carole Pelling

AUNTIE WINNIES' SUNDAY TEA

The room sleeps six days a week
Awakens, stretches and yawns
Its slumbers disturbed by the
Bringing in of Auntie Winnie's Sunday Tea.

Roast Beef laid out between spongy, white sheets
Pickles floating in the vinegar dish
Marshmallows nudging chocolate biscuits off
The gold leaf china plate.

Dust sheets are removed from the Co-op settee
As we take our places around
The 'real coal' electric, two bar heater.
The clock on the wall is glad of some company
To listen to its tick.

But soon Sunday tea will be eaten
Cleared up and put away
The autumn leaf carpet, hoovered
And the best room left to snore away.

Carole Pelling

GOLDFISH BLUES

I would like to be free
And swim in the deepest sea
Perhaps I would end up
As tea, for some bigger fish.
But I would have tasted freedom
And he would have tasted me.

Carole Pelling

DARK IN THE PARK

It's dark in the park
Too early now.
My Mum says,
"Come home at six,
The nights are drawing in."
As if the nights can draw?
Anyway, I HATE staying in.

It is very creepy in the park,
In the dark,
And the night does draw pictures
On the floor and on the walls, of
Scary shadows, that move and bend and dip,
That make my skin shiver.

Mum might just be right and so
I'll go home before six tonight.

Carole Pelling

THE INVISIBLE WOMAN

She leans worn elbows into the windowledge
Hands pushing into sallow cheeks.

No-one ever visits.

She leans, white hair reflecting
The colours of the leaded glass window.

No-one ever visits.

She leans, watching the workers
Scurrying along for the bus into town.

No-one ever visits.

She leans, puckering wrinkled skin,
Watching the children pass at the start of another school day.

No-one ever visits.

She's gone now, died last Tuesday week.
And you'll never guess the numbers of people
Who came to visit,
That empty house
That empty windowledge.

A full house for a funeral tea.

Carole Pelling

MY HERO

He had a lump on his cheek
Told me a tale of a bus that
Had run over his face.
(It was hard to believe)

His hair was made of pure
White cotton with a patch
In the middle where his Maker
had run out of thread.

He wasn't very tall, really
Quite small, perhaps the
Weight of the bus
Had shortened his legs?

His hearing didn't work
When Nan was speaking
But the offer of a
Fish and chip supper
Never went unheard.

He's gone now,
But he's still
MY HERO
There's not many men who
Could stop a bus with their cheek.

Carole Pelling

MISTER PHOTO-GRAPHER MAN

Here mister, have you seen me Mam?
I don't want me photo taken.
I want me Mam and a drink of pop
And a wee and me tea and
What time is the next 67 bus?

Why does he stand in the rain getting
Wet, with that camera?
I don't want me photo taken.
If he doesn't go away
I'll pull a face and he won't want
That in his little photograph.

When me Mam gets back I'll tell
Her about him standing
In front of me, staring and clicking
With the rain dripping off his daft hat.
Hey ... how's that for a silly face
click, click, click, click

'Ere don't you take my face away.

Carole Pelling

SNOW

'Snow' said the weatherman
'Will spread
'Gradually
'Over the whole country — during the night.
'Centimetres of it..
'Inches of it...
'Metres of it...
'In drifts that will cover cars,
'Hide houses,
'Disguise dogs
'And camouflage cows.
'Whole schools will be totally submerged
'As snow continues to fall
'Heavily
'Steadily
'Before turning to rain
'So that by the morning
'The snow will have
'Completely disap

Phil Whitehead

MINAMOTO
YORITOMO'S DREAM

On Snake day (Mi-no-hi)
Minamoto Yoritomo had a
dream
In the dream he drew water
at the spring of Zenairai Benten
and prayed to the deities
by this act the world would
prosper peacefully

Now people come to the spring
to wash their money
for it is believed they will
prosper 7 times 7
Perhaps they will cross over the
small red bridge to the
Turtle Shrine to light incense
sticks – the smoke slowly
spiralling their heavenly
hopes
Some return at a later time
and with new found prosperity
buy a gate for the Temple
Many more are disappointed
their money is clean but
Perhaps they forgot to wash
and purify their souls first
in the clear spring water

Minamoto dreamed of peace
not washi money

Phil Whitehead

In the Hankyu Department Store
Kyoto
A porcelain-pale girl of
great beauty floated
electronically
in
then
out
of my life

escalator
up but
the I
on was
you always
saw going
I down

Phil Whitehead

THE CRACK OF THE SMACK AND THE PATIENT VOICE

(Two views on the discipline of children!)

Crack!
The smack.
Short, sharp, shock waves,
That started somewhere above the knee
But below the bottom,
Travelling, express speed,
Upwards,
Lodging, momentarily
In a part of the brain that
Echoed pain,
With reverse thrust,
Back down to the thigh.
A lifted leg,
A pursed lip,
an intake of breath,
That heaved the tiny chest
In preparation for a sob,
Stifled at once by a second,
Crack!
'And there's another one of those if you start!
I've told you time and again.
Now SIT HERE.'
'Bbut it was an akkcident..'
'Do you want another or not?'

The little girl sobbed behind the windbreak
of stripey blue and green, out of my view.
Her younger sister of 3 or maybe 4, went back to digging the
sandy hole, contented with the blue sky, lapping waves
and the feeling of justice dispensed.

Umi-Chan is very naughty,
Explained her mother, Sumiko.
She always wants things,
And disturbs her sister trying to study.
I have explained to her she must be polite.

Umi-chan sat, like a poppet, on the edge of the huge sofa.
Her eyes round and bright as the darkest, most precious pearls,
Dolls shoes dangling in thin air,
Hands still in her lap.

Umi-chan sat, patiently, for a long time,
Occasionally stealing a glance over at us,
Before Sumiko's laughing voice called to her from the kitchen.

Phil Whitehead

SHARKS IN THE SWIMMING POOL
(subtitled: Piranhas in the Potty)

Part 1:

Sharks in the swimming pool,
Children in the sea.
An unusual arrangement,
Don't you agree.

But strange things occur on mad-summer days
When the sun burns through our ozone-free haze.

(For instance you may find,)

Dog-fish in the cat bowl,
A paddling pool of prawns;
Octopi and limpets
On the hissing summer lawns.

Yes, strange things occur on mad-summer days
When the sprinklers fizzle-out
And the rivers and the streams poison salmon and trout.

Turbot down the toilet,
Kippers in the coke;
Barracudas in the bidet
And that's no joke!

Strange things occur on mad-summer days
When the taps run dry
And the seas are brim full of oil and green slime.

Pike in the Perrier,
Cod in the coffee;
Big surprise for baby—
Piranhas in the potty!

Strange things occur on mad-summer days
When lake water turns to acid
And fish turn violent when their ways are mill-pond placid.

Whales in the whisky,
Sardines in the sink;
Penguins in the pink gin
—Not a drop to drink.

Strange things occur on mad-summer days
When the creatures of the water
Leave ocean, river, lake, to escape the human slaughter.
Where else can they go — their habitat despoiled?
So if I was you when drinking
— I'd always take it boiled.

Phil Whitehead

MORNING POEM

A giant Cornflakes cockerel
crows as the morning dazzles.

The flowers shower colours
against the brightening blue.

Sunburst! –
The day shouts hello.

Rupert M Loydell

PEBBLE

A clenched stone fist
carved by the sea.

Tide brought it to me
on a distant beach:

the sea a line
of crumpled foam

struggling over
the dimpled globe.

Rupert M-Loydell

HOLIDAY SNAPS *(Sark, 1989)*

Swimming in the sea,
the cliff is a wall
in a room of sky.

*

The calf nuzzle-tongues
everyone who goes near.

*

Water palaces
cup rock pools
where you swim.

*

Ten punks pogo together,
throw themselves into the sea.

*

Under moonlight
a hedgehog clatters cutlery
we left outside the tent.

Rupert M Loydell

NGCHOMPHUMSQUASHBLURK
SMELLY
VEHICLE
CLED

DUSTBIN DAY

There are cardboard boxes in the street,
black bags are piled by the door.
The neighbourhood does *not* look neat
when all our rubbish is on the floor.

It's dustbin day, dustbin day,
the day they take all our junk away!

There's a rumble in the street,
and the dustcart trundles round.
We feed the monster garbage
as it makes a hungry sound...

It's dustbin day, dustbin day,
the day they take all our junk away!

"Krang chomp hum squash blurk"
go its teeth at the back.
It eats non-stop, all day long,
sack by plastic sack.

It's dustbin day, dustbin day,
the day they take all our junk away!

Rupert M Loydell

R.I.P.
(Rest In Pieces)

It seems that pedalling wildly
is not the way to ride a bike,
for as Mr. Bugazi came down the hill
he flew over the hedge and out of sight!

The studs on the frame all popped out,
the pedals fell right off —
firstly because of bad driving,
second because of his cough.

He tried to hold it inside,
swallowed back as the tickle came,
but nevertheless, halfway down the road,
it arrived through a throat in pain.

The wheels went all wobbly,
the mudguards shook apart.
Mr. Bugazi coughs no more —
he died of spare bicycle parts.

Rupert M Loydell

If you would like further details of the POEM-SWOP Scheme, send a poem to:

Angela Topping
Poem-Swop Co-Ordinator
11 Beach Grove
Northwich
Cheshire
CW8 1CN

and she'll send you details, a poem-swop and a poem-swop form. It's free, it's helpful and it's fun!